BECOME A SUCCESSFUL VA

ABHI AGARWALA

ABHI AGARWALA

Copyright © 2019 Abhi Agarwala

All rights reserved.

ISBN:9781798991305

DEDICATION

This Book is Dedicated to you, to take a step ahead on your path to success.

CONTENTS

1	Introduction	6
2	Getting Started as a VA	10
3	What type of Jobs a VA Does?	16
4	Where to find work as a VA?	23
5	How to Build your Profile	28
6	Setting your rates	30
7	Where to go from Here...	33
8	About the Author	34

ACKNOWLEDGMENTS

I want to deeply express my gratitude to my uncle Pankaj & Pawan Agarwal, who is always a strong source of support to my life.

I want to express my gratitude to GOD for giving me everything in life.

INTRODUCTION

Have you ever wondered how much money the virtual assistants (VA) make & what type of jobs they typically do? If so, you are not alone. This is one of the rapidly growing industries with tons of work outsourced by small to big companies.

As a VA, you can make money by working from anywhere across the world. So long as you have an Internet connection and a Smartphone or a computer, you can work as a VA.

I wish I had written this book back in the year 2017 when one of my friends was struggling to make good money as a VA so that he could have a smooth transition being a VA. But now he and many other VAs are making more than $3000/month+ and are traveling all around the world, living a digital nomad life.

Hi, my name is Abhi and Co-Founder & CEO of a Facebook specialized advertising company Digital Pexel. I hire VAs for almost all of my work, like data entry, email response, appointment scheduling and more and I was VA even before my journey of entrepreneurship has started.

Most of the companies out there hire a VA for both short-term & long-term projects and you can encash this opportunity. If all of this sounds exciting to you, then read on because I've got a lot more to train you on.

So you might be wondering that all this sounds good, but who exactly is a virtual assistant (VA)?

A virtual assistant (typically abbreviated to VA, also called a virtual office assistant) is a person who provides support services to other businesses from a remote location and provides professional, administrative, technical, or creative (social) assistance to the clients remotely from home or own office and not from the client's location.

It's a win-win situation for both you and your clients, as you being a VA can charge variable pricing from client to client depending on your skills and client's project. Whereas the client is also benefited from virtual assistants as VAs are independent contractors rather than employees. Clients are not responsible for any employee-related taxes, insurance or benefits, except in the context that those indirect expenses are included in the VAs fees.

These days, clients also avoid the logistical problem of providing extra office space, equipment or supplies. Clients pay for 100% productive work and can work with virtual assistants individually, or in multi-VA firms to meet their exact needs.

What does a Virtual Assistant Do?

You might be thinking that it sounds great to me but does a VA actually do? The answer is pretty simple; anything that is done online can be done by a VA.

A VA can do anything that's done by support except bringing a coffee ;)

Here are some examples of work that a VA can do:

- Data Entry
- Social Media Management
- Writing
- Editing
- Proofreading
- Podcast Editing
- Transcription
- Graphics Design (most VA uses Canva, no special skill require)
- Project Management
- Email Support
- Event Planning
- Web Designing.
- Web Management
- Content Uploading
- Payroll
- Human Resources
- Coaching
- Internet Research
- Consulting
- Phone-Call Management
- Excel
- Copywriting
- Budgets/Accounting
- And much more!

As you can see, there are many jobs a VA can help with.

So, if all these make sense to you and you want to know how to get started, keep reading and I will guide you step-by-step how you can start as a VA.

GETTING STARTED AS A VA

You might be wondering how to do I get started as a VA? Actually, there are very basic requirements to get started as a VA but let's check them one by one. First, you will require a computer and an Internet Connection to get connected to a client. Secondly, you need to select a niche. Niche means what type of services you want to offer as a VA. You can offer any type of services as a VA, which may vary from data entry to business consulting but I would suggest not to opt for too many tasks at one time.

The reason is twofold; first, you'll burn out too quickly if you try to provide too many services. Secondly, you'll not be able to establish yourself as an authority or an expert in few selected niches.

As a VA you can even charge a premium price, like $35-$50/hour only if you have a specifically defined skill set that you have practiced over time and are comfortable doing it.

Let me show you one example of how the VAs get paid based on the service they provide.

Upwork

Typical Rates Charged by Virtual Assistants*

Type of Virtual Assistant	Description	Average Hourly Rate
Administrative Professional/Data Entry VA	Proofreading, data entry, clerical work, research, Excel, etc.	$12-20+
Marketing VA/Customer Service/Accounting Support	Copywriting, budgets/accounting, marketing support, customer support, CRM software experience, email marketing, social media marketing, software like PowerPoint, Quickbooks, Salesforce, WordPress, etc	$20-35+
Advanced VA/Consultant Executive Assistant	Business consulting, content management, project management, advanced IT/site management, web development, and server management	$38-50+

*Reflect rates charged by freelancers on Upwork in North America with over 1,000 hours and 90% success rate.

This data has been provided by Upwork, one of the world's most trusted freelancing site.

As you can see that there are the different types of services that a VA provides and they get paid accordingly:

- ☐ Administrative Professional/ Data Entry VA:
    - ☐ Proofreading
    - ☐ Data Entry
    - ☐ Clerical work
    - ☐ Excel, etc.

    This type of VA typically charges an average hourly rate: $12-20+/hour.

- ☐ Marketing VA/Customer Service/Accounting Support:
    - ☐ Copywriting
    - ☐ Budgets/Accounting.
    - ☐ Marketing Support
    - ☐ Customer Support

- ☐ CRM Software Experience
- ☐ Email Marketing
- ☐ Social Media Marketing
- ☒ Software like PowerPoint, Quickbooks, Salesforce, WordPress, etc.

This type of VA typically charges an average hourly rate: $20-35+/hour.

- ☐ Advanced VA/Consultant, Executive Assistant:
  - ☐ Business Consulting
  - ☐ Content Management
  - ☐ Project Management
  - ☐ Advanced IT/site Management
  - ☐ Web Development
  - ☐ Server Management , etc.

This type of VA typically charges an average hourly rate: $38-50+/hour.

Besides, VA charges based on the service they provide, the expertise they gain over time.

The above image also shows the hourly rate of VAs who have worked for more than 1000s of hours, but that's not the usual case if you already have a specific set of skills or if you are providing very specific service, you can charge premium amount as a VA.

That's why I highly suggest you select a specific service that you want to offer as a VA.

Now once you have decided what services you want to offer as a VA, the next question that arises is where to Find Clients who can hire you as a VA?

Disclaimer: Many people have this dogma that they need to be an expert in the services they provide as a VA; however it's not true in most of the cases. You can start providing any type of service as a VA just by doing 30-60 minutes of research on a particular topic. Many times when somebody hires a VA, they train the VA in a step-by-step manner on how to execute the things in a specific format. So relax, choose something that you are already comfortable with or would like to learn about.

Now, where to Find Clients who can hire you as a VA:

There are some sites that I would prefer. I know that many people get confused at this stage but you don't have to worry about it. I am always there to back you up. In fact, it's one of the most exciting ways for you to get your hands dirty as a VA ;)

There are some sites that I would highly suggest you start with if you are a complete newbie or starting as a fresher. These sites will provide you with better exposure and will help you build up a good portfolio over time.

Sites you can use to find VA work:

- UpWork (Highly Recommended)
- Freelancer
- PeoplePerHour

- Guru
- HireMyMom
- Zirtual
- Uassit.Me
- 123Employee
- Worldwide101
- 24/7 virtual assistant
- LongerDays

I would suggest instead of registering on all these sites, just start with 2-3 sites or max 4 sites which suit you the best. Begin by filling in your profile details for each one. Be sure to include the type of work you are looking for, it will make easy for you to find the right client. I will be talking more about it in detail later on.

Also, one key skill required to succeed in any work is to have perseverance or persistence, anything good you do will require these two critical skills for you to succeed. If you face any issue feel free to tweet me or follow me at twitter, I'll try my best to help you out. Like you all, I have my own share of mistakes but I always try to focus on the solution instead of the problem and that's what I'm expecting from you.

KEYNOTE

WHAT TYPE OF JOBS DOES A VA HANDLE?

I think I have made this point clear in Chapter 1 regarding the type of Jobs a VA typically does. Most of the virtual assistant work falls inside the 3 verticals:

- ☐ Administrative Professionals/ Data Entry VA: The VA who works under this category typically earns anywhere between $12-20/hour.
- ☐ Marketing VA/Customer Service/Accounting Support: The VA who works under this category typically earns anywhere between $20-$35/hour.
- ☐ Advanced VA/Consultant, Executive Assistant: The VA who works under this category typically earns anywhere between $38-$50/hour.

There are a few points I would like to mention before you start your journey as a virtual assistant:

- The rate may be more or less, depending on the skills of the VA and the type of project they are working on.
- The rate may also vary depending on their success ratio and past projects.
- The rate of a VA may also depend on the region from where he is providing his service, like for the same project a VA from North America can charge an hourly rate of $25/hour but VA from Philippines or India may only able charge $10-15/hour (This is just

observation, actual hourly rate may vary depending on the skills of freelancers)

As a VA you have flexibility in choosing the options. This will help you narrow down the services that you are most qualified to perform. If you are starting as a newbie, start with something you are most comfortable at. Don't go for any job that you find, rather stick to your selected services that you find you are comfortable offering.

One key aspect that I like most about being a VA is that if you have some interest or knowledge about any field, you can do more research, learn new things in that area and charge even premium pricing for your specific skills.

It's always better to master a specific set of skills and offer that as a service to your client.

Though the list of services that you can offer as a VA is endless, however, I would suggest you, focus on some popular tasks that you can choose as a virtual assistant.

Some of these could be:

- WordPress Post Publishing:

    One of the easiest jobs a VA can do is to publish and maintain content on the WordPress Site.

    WordPress is one of the simplest CMS (Content Management System) platforms that do not require any HTML or CSS knowledge to maintain the site.

Many Bloggers hire a VA for their day to day task like post publishing, optimizing an existing post, adding images and more.

The best thing I like about WordPress is that you can like everything in WordPress in 60 minutes or less even if you're not a tech-savvy guy.

- [ ] Email Management:

One thing that I have observed these days is that most companies outsource is their email support. Every company receives tons of emails and they need to reply to their customer in order to make them happy and satisfied. For this, they simply don't have the in-house resource to handle all their customer responses and that's when they hire a VA for their work.

The role of a VA in Email management is to reply to the customer queries. If there are any specific issues, forward it to the concerned team and so on. And the best part is that it does not require any superpower.

- [ ] Writing & Editing:

If you are good at writing or even have basic writing skills and a willingness to learn, this is an excellent way to make money online as a virtual assistant.

Today's there are more than 152 million blogs on the internet and many bloggers out their needs your help desperately.

Many successful bloggers run more than 2 to 3 or even more blogs. They know that the only way to magnetize consistent traffic to their blog is by producing high-quality content and keeping their audience engaged. And for that, they don't have sufficient time to produce quality content and even if they do have the time, they still need someone who can edit their blog before it gets ready to be published online.

Many bloggers even hire a VA to write a catchy headline, as a magnetic headline gets the maximum number of clicks.

☐ Editorial Calendar:

An Editorial Calendar is crucial for managing successful blogs on the Internet. You as a VA are expected to maintain the editorial calendar, keep the content up to date that needs to be published in a specific time. You need to come up with fresh ideas that you can pin on the editorial board (virtually) and update your publisher/content creator about the calendar and more.

☐ Social Media Management (SMM):

Social media is booming and all types of businesses ranging from small to big companies use social media to create and maintain their online presence. In fact, the U.S. alone spend more than $70B (yes comes with a B-billion) in the year 2018 on digital marketing activities.

What does this mean to you? It simply means you are sitting on a gold mine. I have seen many VAs who have already made a good amount of money only through managing social media accounts for their clients.

So, you might be thinking about what are the roles that you can fit into as a Social media manager?

Let me specify a few of the key roles that you can fit into as a social media manager. You will be responsible for curating social media content. Curating the content is different from creating it.

Suppose I am a blogger and I have published blog content, now I want to promote it. So for different social media accounts, I want to curate specific content. Let's say I am promoting my content on Pinterest. In this case, the graphics for promoting on Pinterest will be different from when promoting on Facebook. So as a VA, your responsibility will be to curate content for different social media platforms.

Along with it, you will also be responsible for scheduling the social media posts, creating social media calendar (like hootsuite, buffer, hubspot & more) besides replying to social media messages. Some more key responsibilities include deleting spam, acting as a moderator on platforms like Facebook and much more.

If you are more into Social Media this can be a perfect role for you.

- ☐ Graphic Design:

If you more of a creative person then this is one of the most profitable ways to encash your creativity as a virtual assistant. If you are skilled at Photoshop or just want to learn online design or graphic design, this is the field you would seriously want to consider diving into.

The best part is that it doesn't require you to be an excellent graphic designer. You can create beautiful graphics or pins, just by using one of the simplest sites known as Canva. I feel that you can start creating beautiful graphics without having complex Photoshop skills in Canva by just investing 60-90 minutes of your learning time from blogs or YouTube. People out there are ready to take money out of their wallet in exchange for your graphics work.

Now you might be thinking if it is so easy why don't people do it by themselves? Actually, it is a valid question!

It is simply because people don't have the skills, time or most importantly the desire to do it by themselves. If you feel that there is a child or artist who is passionate about design, I would strongly recommend this skillset.

Please note, this is only an overview of some of the work that a VA does and there is a lot more alloyed to it.

Now that you have learned what type of work a VA does, I think you might have also given a thought regarding the type of services you want to offer as a virtual assistant. Now let's shine some torch on more details regarding where you can find the right client for your work.

WHERE TO FIND WORK AS A VA?

As I have mentioned before, that there are several sites that you can consider joining which suits you the best but in this chapter, I would like to go a little bit deeper so that you can get better clarity about what type of jobs you should apply as a virtual assistant. Also, I think that I have made it clear till now that you don't need a superpower to become a good VA ;).

Let us also check the sites that I mentioned earlier where you can go to find work as a VA:

- UpWork (Highly Recommended)
- Freelancer
- PeoplePerHour
- Guru
- HireMyMom
- Zirtual
- Uassit.Me
- 123Employee
- Worldwide101
- 24/7 virtual assistant
- LongerDays

So, there are two ways to becoming a High Paying VA. One is the Inbound Process and the other one is an Outbound Process. Let's discuss both one by one and how you can apply for those processes to get high paying VA jobs.

Inbound Process

This is not a typical Inbound Process that you see in the content marketing world where people visit your site and offer a job but it's almost similar to that. It is the process of registering yourself on several VA sites and applying for the work that you feel most comfortable doing.

For the sake of explaining, I am going to take the example of UpWork. It's also one of the best freelancing sites out there. I believe that by now you have got some clarity as to what you want to offer as your service.

Once you go to upwork.com, in the search bar, enter the categories of the jobs that you want to apply for. Let's say I want to apply for "social media management".

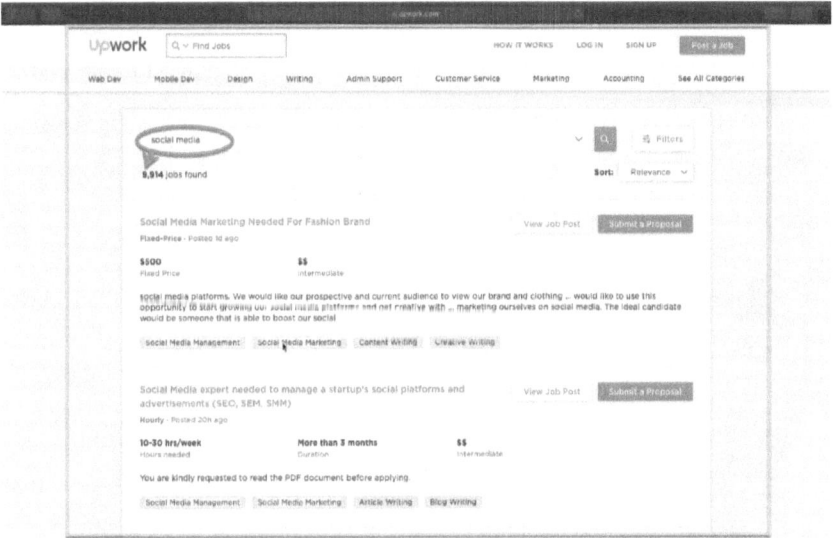

As you can see that, for the search term "social media" it is showing 9,914 jobs available at the time of creating this content and the jobs keep getting updated every minute.

So, out of 9,914 jobs available for social media marketing, you need to read the job description very carefully because it can tell you more about the client, his work and whether you are a perfect fit for the job or not. Don't just apply to any job, read it carefully before applying.

After reading everything about the job description if you feel you are a good fit, apply for the job but use reverse engineering to make your proposal stand out amongst your competitors.

One cool little hack that I want to share with you is that when applying for a job, always greet the client by his or her name. By default, UpWork doesn't show you the client name until he or she accepts your proposal. So how to know the client's name? Catch-22 ;)

You can know a potential client's name just by browsing through the previous feedback that he or she got from other freelancers, below the job description. It always makes a difference to have a human touch and please make sure that you send a personalized proposal for the job you are applying to. An experienced client can easily sense the "canned proposal" and they reject the proposal almost instantly.

This information will help you choose the best client and make a better connection with them for ongoing or long-term projects.

Outbound Process

This process is like reaching out to potential business people and offering your service to them.

Once you have got clarity on the type of services you want to offer as a VA, don't feel afraid to go out and ask the business people if they need any help in a particular area of their business.

You can create a post on your social media platform asking if someone is interested in availing your service or if anyone needs any help in the type of service that you are providing as a VA.

Let me share a ninja technique with you, what you can employ to get a few initial responses. You can connect with many potential LinkedIn and Facebook Groups and deliver people value first.

If they are looking for something, go research on their problem, help them in advance and ask them later on if they want your service. You can even offer 2-3 days of trial or even a week of the trial to showcase your service. After that, if you both feel you are a good fit for one another, you can carry on from there. But no matter whether you are a beginner or an intermediate, always make sure that you do not charge below $10-$15/hour. Do your research on freelancing sites regarding what type of hourly rate you should charge based on the service that you offer and the value you provide.

Always have confidence while communicating with your potential client that you are offering some valuable service to them that will surely help them in their business.

LinkedIn is a key platform to reach out to the potential decision makers, only make sure not to waste their time. None of the influential people like to read a wall of text, be straight to the point. Always and always be humble while communicating, as it can lead to long-term opportunities and even that potential prospect can refer you to other potential guys who are in need of your service. Before making a connection, be sure to know more about their business, work ethics, business models and more. Decision makers like bloggers and entrepreneurs like to work with people who can understand their vision and business.

HOW TO BUILD YOUR PROFILE TO GET MORE WORK AS A VA.

Now that you have learned something about the services you want to offer, where to find your potential clients? Now it's time to showcase them your skills.

And the best way to showcase your skills or services that you want to offer to your client in order to charge good hourly pay is to have your decent website. On your website mention about your services, basic info, your contact info, how people can approach you, your passion for your work, why you do what you do, etc.

What if you don't have any portfolio to showcase to your client? In that case, I would suggest to create your blog around the topic you want to serve as a virtual assistant.

It will serve a two-fold purpose. One, it will show your passion for your service area to your potential prospect. Second, it will help you to gain traffic to your site that will help you monetize your site through ads, affiliate marketing and more.

Suppose you want to become a "Social Media management" VA. So either you can show your past project that you have done for the previous client or you can start writing content around social media management like "Top 10 Twitter best practices", "How to get more Instagram followers" and more.

To accomplish the above objective i.e. to have your own website, you will need two things. First, is to have a domain name that you can get from Namecheap for $10 or less. Second, I would suggest you, get a domain hosting. I would highly recommend Bluehost hosting, as they are the BEST in the market and also at the same time inexpensive.

For the domain name, I would suggest going with your own name as a brand that you can showcase to your potential client or going for a name that is related to your service. Be sure to research and verify if the name is available in the different social media platforms.

Once again, keep your website simple to showcase the previous work you have done for your client or any client testimonial or even creating your own blog to display a passion for your service area and generate money out of it.

SETTING YOUR RATES

From the very beginning of the book, I made it clear that setting up your rate correctly is one of the key aspects that will help you to win the VA game.

Even if you are starting at day 1 as a VA, don't quote your pricing below $10/hour or you will always be overwhelmed and wonder why you started as a VA in the first place. Therefore, it is important to not sell yourself short.

I usually notice that many new VAs undercut their value because they don't have any idea of pricing and how to charge accordingly. And most of them even fear that if they charge a decent hourly rate they will lose the client. While it may be true that you will lose some client on the upfront but it's even good for you as these clients don't deserve your work if they aren't willing to pay you at least $10/hour.

I pay anywhere between $10-25/hour depending on the nature of the work.

If you quote low hourly rate charges as a VA, you will always feel distressed and burnt out too quickly. You will never feel satisfied with the returns.

Luckily you don't have to fall into that dogma of uncertainty and undervalue yourself as I have already shared the pricing structure for the different type of work that a VA does. Let's see for one more time:

Type of Virtual Assistant	Description	Average Hourly Rate
Administrative Professional/Data Entry VA	Proofreading, data entry, clerical work, research, Excel, etc.	$12-20+
Marketing VA/Customer Service/Accounting Support	Copywriting, budgets/accounting, marketing support, customer support, CRM software experience, email marketing, social media marketing, software like PowerPoint, Quickbooks, Salesforce, WordPress, etc.	$20-35+
Advanced VA/Consultant Executive Assistant	Business consulting, content management, project management, advanced IT/site management, web development, and server management	$38-50+

*Reflect rates charged by freelancers on Upwork in North America with over 1,000 hours and 90% success rate.

You can use the above image as a baseline for your work so that you don't feel confused even as a beginner.

No doubts you can compromise with the pricing only to build your portfolio and to get a few initial clients. However, once you have gained the expertise in your services, be sure to charge according to the market rate and even more if you are having great communication skill and understanding with your clients.

None of the potential clients would like to let you go if you fit great in their working culture. They know that if they would let you go, they will need to hire another VA and train him or her once again from scratch that will consume their own time. So make sure you deliver excellent work to your existing client so that when you demand an increase in your hourly rate they don't need to think twice.

Also, once you develop your skills with time you can charge premium amount, means if you are jumping from your hourly rate of $10/hour to $20/hour, you can work less, have more freedom and earn more money in less time.

Always remember that if some client asks you to compromise in your pricing, just say a big "NO" and walk away. Remember that for one project that you say no to, there's someone else who is willing to give you a well deserving project.

Once you take any project be sure to be responsive to your client msgs and keep them updated about your work & if you're unsure what type of work, a client is expecting from you be sure to make it clear before you commit to a project. In this way, you will able to retain your client and build a healthy relation with your client.

WHERE TO GO FROM HERE...

I (Abhi Agarwala) would like to personally say a big "THANK YOU" from the bottom of my heart for taking out time and learning something effective that can help you make $1000, $2000 or even $5000+ as a virtual assistant.

Today's world is full of opportunities; the only problem is that people don't act on them. I wish you a great success ahead in the future.

Be patient, don't give up to too early, work steadily, deliver high-quality work and you will see results you want to see as a virtual assistant.

Track your time that you are devoting and projects that you are orchestrating for your client. What gets measured gets improved! Try to have good communication with other VAs as this can be a lonely journey.

The only last tip-offs that I want to share with you is that believe in yourself, do hard work and you will see the results. If you really work hard, build your portfolio and build a connection with good potential clients, being a virtual assistant is something that can change your life forever.

Wish you a great success ahead... :)

ABOUT THE AUTHOR

Abhi Agarwala is the founder of "Digital Pexel" a Facebook and Instagram Specialized Marketing Company where he and his team work closely with many E-commerce, Insurance, and U.S. & U.K. clients.

Mr. Abhi is also a Growth Consultant where he provides mentorship to professional people having 10+ years of experience. He helps them to unlock their hidden potential and become unstoppable.

Abhi believes that anyone can achieve success where he's now, they only need to model what he had learned throughout the years.

What started as a passion soon converted into a burning desire to help 100,000 students & Entrepreneurs live an Internet Lifestyle life where they can work from any time, anywhere they want.

Abhi is a 27 year old coach, trainer, entrepreneur and a conscious mentor where he not only help his tribe members to install a specific set of skills required to live a desired lifestyle but at the same time, train them to raise over their mental, emotional and physical challenges and become the best version of themselves.

Read more about Abhi Agarwala & Signup for my small email series at ABHIAGARWALA.COM that will help you achieve next level of greatness :)

Your Fan,

Abhi "A Human Being in Progress" Agarwala

www.ingramcontent.com/pod-product-compliance
Lightning Source LLC
Chambersburg PA
CBHW031515210526
45464CB00007B/2916